Colorfast

Part 2

The Meter is Irregular

Volume 5

Roddy

1st WORLD PUBLISHING

Colorfast, Part 2

The Meter is Irregular, Volume 5

Roddy

Copyright © 2020 Rodney Charles

Published by 1st World Publishing
P.O. Box 2211, Fairfield, Iowa 52556
tel: 641-209-5000 • fax: 866-440-5234
web: www.1stworldpublishing.com

First Edition

Library of Congress Cataloging-in-Publication Data.
ISBN: 978-1-4218-3645-4

This material has been written and published for educational purposes to enhance one's well-being. In regard to health issues, the information is not intended as a substitute for appropriate care and advice from health professionals, nor does it equate to the assumption of medical or any other form of liability on the part of the publisher or author. The publisher and author shall have neither liability nor responsibility to any person or entity with respect to loss, damages, or injury claimed to be caused directly or indirectly by any information in this book.

for Nandini

More memories...

Don't let me carry on
babbling nonsense
like a child
overstuffed with caramel and cola.

Like you, I suffer the consequences
of American extravagance —
senses clogged with undigested stimulation,
layer upon layer of grey
anesthetic vibrations.

Hearing everything but silence,
tasting everything without appetite,
seeing the world, blood red,
with preconceptions
propaganda and dogma —
exhaustions.

Slap my face.
Discipline me.
Turn me back the other way.

This is the force of love,
the force of karma,
there is no difference.

What draws us to each other
obeys no quantum laws —
it's barely reasonable at all.

What attracts us?
What divides us?
Help me with these little details.

~

I married you,
the third time,
in Canada —
Regina
Justice of the Peace,
a small oak office
perfumed with hundred-year-old paper,

poorly ventilated.
You wore white —
a dress we bought a few days earlier
and tailored to your child-like figure.

Like tambourines, we tapped in time
with the mumblings of the magistrate —
I take you to be my lawfully wedded everything...

Again,
time stops,
allowing me to glance history —
what steered us here?

~

1991
American Gallery of Vedic Art

Remember
our early days —
our first proposal?
You said *no*,
but I didn't believe you.

You said I couldn't hear you.
You said I was a dreamer
and offered me a catalogue of reasons.
But it was not the voice of wholeness I
heard,
it was a child fretting about toys and play-
things —
No concealed a *Yes*.

You needed time,
time to finish telling your story,
so I left for Jaipur,
wounded but assured.

Whatever you were searching for,
you found it in yourself.
No became *Yes*
and *Yes* exploded,
obliterating our old stories,
the Milky Way,
its stars and planets,
repositioning our souls.

We put a ring on your finger
and listened
to hear a new voice singing —
two unlikely voyagers,
both affirming,
come in, and don't mind the sparks.

A date was set.
You said two weeks.
I said nine months.
Two weeks later, we wed —
first time, New Delhi.

A fourteen-day marathon began
in the haze of that foggy night:

√ ~ Soar from Delhi to Amsterdam,
      thirty thousand feet.
√ ~ Supply commissioned
      chef-d'oeuvre to buyers in Holland.
√ ~ Forty hours, depart for Chicago,
      thirty-two thousand feet.
√ ~ Disembark, unload

√ ~ Lease a Windy City van, plain white
(lowest rate)

√ ~ Whoosh, a blur to Fairfield,

√ ~ Implore Henderson's Custom Framing
to mat, mount and case sixty Indian
originals in three unreasonable days.

Swiftly,

Dash,

√ ~ Thirteen hundred homeward miles to
snow-coated Canada —

begging family excuse-me's for such a
hasty wedding.

√ ~ Whoosh, a blur, return to Fairfield —
overloaded — fine art

√ ~ Cram framed and matted masters
in a basic white, Windy City van —
rocketing to Manhattan

√ ~ Hustle booths 101 and 102 —
Art Expo America.

Fifty-six hours of salesmanship,

√ ~ Reload the Windy City — near empty
now, a triumph

√ ~ Road-trip home,
a blur to Fairfield,

√ ~ Confirm Texas; Spring exhibit,
√ ~ Race to O'Hare
√ ~ United Airlines 86
    "now departing for New Delhi, India",
    thirty-six thousand feet.

Touchdown in fog,
within, without,
our first joining ceremony
begins at noon.

~

Marrying?
Jetlagged?
Don't let me carry on
babbling again,
like a new groom

Slap my face
and discipline me.
Turn me the other way.
My words may make you sleepy,
but there is more, much more —

who else will join this unexpected
companionship?

~

No one can help me
when my memories wash ashore,
shipwrecked,
but I can't resist picking up every splinter,
in any order, it doesn't matter.
The ocean is so deep
and waves never cease.

~

It took three days,
maybe four,
to properly marry us.

I remember your essence
near me,
almost always there, on my left side,
with a sacred fire in front of us
and a lovely stream of family and friends

blessing us with folded hands, kind words,
damp eyes, rare colognes and extraordinary
perfumes.

Before the marriage assembly,
with stuffed bowls of raw white rice,
sweet fruits, camphor, sandalwood,
crisp morning flowers, burnished silk cloth
and seven pilgrim crossings, circling the
fire —
generation after generation emerging,
pure or impure,
peering out from the flames
in great relief
to see stars and planets,
the vacuum of space,
music, wisdom and laughter,
kingdoms of sunlight and azure skies,
lyrics, harmonies
and five hundred thousand miles of
roadway,
gambling everything.

~

No one told us,
but we knew —
the wedding fire consumed our old life,
scorched our identities
and laid us flat, disoriented
and frankly exhausted.

Marriage-fire is a magician
transforming grooms and brides
to faceted mirrors —revealing only our own
reflection.

For twenty-six years,
I put my lips next to your cheek
on hearing the sound of your sweet music —
mindful that I am a guest in your arms,
mindful that I have been forgetful, every
minute.

As these words appear,
I wonder,
can you feel—
everything today
is for you?

~

Remember
the abandoned stone temple somewhere near
Udaipur,
where your soul heard something from my
soul?

There was a baby calf in a nearby stable,
all alone,
longing to play with us.

She must have heard something too,
because she galloped around us
with new purpose,
fearless and strong,
strutting and nudging
to the beat of inner poetry.

Standing settled,
side by side,
our fingers brushed lightly.
An electric blue pulse, magnetic,
leaped from hand to hand,

back and forth
like a competent ballerina
stealing breath from a spellbound critic.

Like you,
the earth
holds a charge deep inside herself.
She sings to the clouds
and draws their threatening voltage
into her heart.
It's a game they play,
mother and child.
The toddler shows his mighty power
and the mother surrenders her treasure —
sustenance,
balance,
the force of love, or karma —
there is no difference.

~

Remember
Canoeing
the Colorado River in Austin?

We tried so hard to
sneak up on free-floating river logs
speckled with Texas Cooters,
warming their tiny heads and feet
like sunflowers at noon.

Texas turtles are in no hurry —
they yield a royal pace,
knowing —
there is no place to be
that's not home.

So much drama,
so many stories of grief,
but the real chitchat is;
inside the shell
there is no drama at all,
just a turtle
who never leaves the premises.

We watched the sunset that evening —
gold transformed to ruby,
you squeezed my hand and exhaled,
"So beautiful!"

Inside my shell,
I whispered,
"Bugsy—
It's the joy of being opened."

~

Remember
Major League baseball
Texas Rangers
Arlington Stadium—
fallen popcorn burying our sandaled feet?
We teased our hosts—
"slowest game ever".

You sat so close to me,
I thought you were cold.
I stole a quick kiss.
You reluctantly surrendered
your public modesty.

Shouts came in and out,
strike, ball, hit,
but you only heard me
and I only knew you.

22

The ocean surged
in the heat of middle afternoon,
a picnic of sounds and smells
congested the humid air.
I saw the flash in your eyes—
a need for water.
I touched your skin
so you could be yourself
and the waves pulled you back to the ocean
again,
away from dry land,
back to the moment
where you first learned—
the Milky Way never stops flowing.

Don't worry,
water is always somewhere.

~

I've seen that look in your eyes before—
"Do I love you"?
It bothers you when I laugh so hard,
but I mean no affront.

I laugh because there is nothing left of me.
Your stars have consumed my old life —
there is no resistance.
But knock if you must,
or ring the bell,
I'll open the door
as I always do,
with assurance.

~

Remember
Yellowstone —
rivers of geyser hot steam and glacier cold
water
commingling to a single whistling torrent
of perfect hot-springs water?

Love opened my chest
and an evening star disappeared into it,
urgently longing for a song —
a buoyant melody nature invents
when she reveals herself.
How can she be lonesome

when her echo pulsates everywhere,
connecting everything to everything?

~

Remember
Dragon's Mouth
near Wyoming's Mud Volcano?

She lived up to her name —
Her lashing forked tongue,
belching fanged waves of steam and boiling
muck
from her cavernous jaw
in perfect pulse
with the volcanic monster below,
counting each moment,
an embryo simmering,
soon reborn,
steady, like Old Faithful —

Unknowing tourists
on winding boardwalks,
are parade ants,

defiantly insensible
to Smaug's restless slumber
just inches below their feet,
dreaming of atomic ash, plums, and hellfire,
impatiently smoldering
with dreams of obliteration.

But the sun is high
and fear
is meaningless—
existence obliterates existence,
then thrives
to create more existence.

~

Do you remember the buried treasure
on Mount Athabasca?
Our fearless four-year-old
set a pace to the summit
that left us far behind.
Your frozen head,
wrapped in a turban of
children's underwear,

absolutely ridiculous,
captured my admiration.

We collected our quarters,
dimes and nickels
and hid them in a hole,
hopeful that future family explorers
would uncover them
and household stories of laughter, mirth
and unexpected treasure
would live on
and multiply.

~

Again,
my mind wonders.
I'm floating in real-time.

You're in Agra today.
Gone 23 days, so far.
I'm alone in Fairfield,
longing to be there.

It's a dance we do,
but I'll sit there with you
at the Taj Mahal
on a marble bench,
hand in hand,
with our faces
cheek to cheek.

Wondering,
I remember
the first love story I read—
The Profit by Kahlil Gibran.

The minute I heard it,
I searched everywhere for you,
not knowing how foolish that was.

An eye is meant to see
what's in front of it.
A soul is meant for love
and nothing more.
Gibran had lit a fire
that burned everything.
I had no idea

that on the way to you,
many years and miles and
dangers and delusions
would come stampeding in
like cattle frightened by a thunderbolt.

But what piles up outside
is guided by the mining inside,
unearthing the clues, the signs, the symbols,
the meaning of concealed memories
and the reason Gibran was born with sparks
to spread a fire
so far North in a frozen Canadian winter
to a child of fourteen,
for whom India seems so far away
and yet, altogether familiar.

~

Remember
Uncle Julian?

Like Mother,
he lost everything made of clay.

The dark shame of World War II
stole their father, mother and childhood,
but not honorability.

Standing alone
in a sea of sorrows,
holding tight to a broken family,
his heart was scoured dirt-free
like infant's laughter at new delights.

His smile hid no secrets,
His open-mouthed laugh said, "You are safe."
I knew he loved me
because I could see he loved himself.

Like my Mother,
he was blessed with restless energy —
Chronic chatterboxes, both of them.
When no one would listen,
they would hum
and fix whatever was broken.

He understood simplicity,
and why it mattered most of all,

why no lie is ever really hidden from view
and how small betrayals of the mind
can lead to shadowy, dark empires
of misguided followers, too frightened to
lose everything made of clay.

He knew the purpose of happiness
and easily made my young soul sing
by being inquisitive about everything
and routinely toasting his own
brilliant conclusions.

Like my Mother,
he was a bull,
unyielding,
some might say stubborn —
but a bull once shattered his spine.

A full body cast immobilized him for a year.
Doctors assured him he was disabled.

But he knew the reason he was happy,
and realized doctors knew little about bulls,
their strength, their will, their self-reliance

and how much easier it would be
to repair a broken, shattered body
than resist the small betrayals of the mind
that silently grow to be shadowy, dark empires.

Fully recovered,
he became a rancher once again,
humbly proud of his record-breaking one-
armed pushups
for which he challenged me at every oppor-
tunity.
My highest accomplishment: Almost 1.
I may be exaggerating by about ¼.

He was a cowboy.
Remember I used to tell you stories of my
childhood summers—
How my uncle let me sleep in the
bunkhouse with the other cowboys
and taught me how to groom,
ride and love a horse?

He understood the cowhand's unspoken
esteem,
and recognized the illusion of time—

how few ever see
a hundred springs,
a hundred summers,
a hundred winters,
a hundred cattle drives,
beyond the natural limit
and why no regrets,
or wide-mouthed apologies
could ever be the legacy
of cowboys blessed with natal gratitude.

Like my mother,
he was a bull,
he was happy
and he knew why.

Some days,
I kiss the ground,
grateful for a lineage
of bulls,
grandmother to great, great, grandfather
practicing straightforwardness,
cherishing simplicity
and knowing why.

Like my mother and uncle,
I am self-proud,
thoughtful that no lie remains hidden
from view,
conscious that small betrayals
can lead to shadowy dark empires
of misguided factions.

They taught me — be happy,
celebrate and toast incurable curiosity,
cultivate courage,
be equipped to lose everything made of clay.

My Mother lived.
My uncle lived.
They acknowledge me as part of them.
What else matters?
It's intrinsic and beyond calculation.

As a toddler, my mother taught me a song
—merrily, merrily, merrily, merrily,
life is but a dream.
Life is but a dream —
Life is but a dream —

Measured from every critical angle,
this lilting dream
appears real
for those asleep or drunk —
and one day,
we wake up.

~

Drifting again
I ask myself,
"Am I a hypocrite?
What trials have I suffered?"

A gentle inside voice answers,
"Don't worry, you'll pay plenty for
your mistakes."

I am comforted,
knowing I'll be debt-free.

Likewise,
I am heartened,
knowing death is my trusted friend
—so far.

Death,
affable,
loves an honest poem
and waits willingly,
without effort,
unwearyingly,
'til one day,
I author one.

What happens when you rub life and death
together?

I tease you frequently,
saying, "We are polar opposites",
but wasn't Robert Clausius right?
"Energy is neither created nor destroyed,
just transformed"?
~(Second Law of Thermodynamics)

It's not nice to tease hurtfully.
That's not my intention.
It's my way of being funny,
my way of saying that
when you mix hot with cold,
expect transformation.

Again, I probe,
what happens when you rub life and death
together?
—perfect balance?

Don't worry,
seductive death,
my right-hand friend
who loves an honest poem,
is patiently anticipating my debut.

~

Who can repay my friendly friend—
faithful death?

She teases me daily.

"Wake up, Charles.
Time to rise, Charles.
Let's go, Charles.
There is enough time for sleep
in thy grave, Charles.

Face your wolves now, Charles,
they'll grow in force and number —
Fight, Charles."

Today,
the dust of civilizations,
long forgotten,
is piled high upon my conscience.

Did we really begin as minerals —
a primordial bouillabaisse?

How many enumerable transformations
have we known?
Whose keeping track?

A gentle voice replies,
"Like birthday parties,
do we really remember them all?"

This poem is not round.
Like a star, it has many points
and many happy endings,
and Faithful Death

holds my hand to give life
to them all.

"I am right here, Charles.
Fight like a starving shark, Charles.
Fight for friendliness, compassion, happi-
ness,
sights, sounds and words,
kind acts,
tears and precious love.
Fight for courage.
Fight like a fuming bull, Charles.

Fight until your hands fall limp, Charles,
then, I'll depart no more."

About the Author

(Saskatchewan Borealis)

I was young
When the never-failing flame of Queen
City's oil refinery
Blazed both eerie and calming
At once

Like losing individuality

I never imagined
One day
The open sky would consume every memory
Changing crude to gasoline
Like the gravity of love

My close friends tell me
I've spent too many Canadian winters
Freezing neurons

They're right
And that's how I know
They're honest souls

But my own wolf pack
Saskatchewan bred
Discovered new verses
Remembering the kindred love
Piercing our bodies supine
The night we lay
Hand in hand
Vulnerable and exposed
Eyes to the stars
Bathed in aurora

And that first kiss
From which I've never recovered

Other Books by Rodney Charles

Every Day a Miracle Happens
Lighter Than Air
Publish It Now
Book Marketing Basics
Miracles of the Saints
The Land of Love Art and Genius
The Secret Meaning of Names

The Meter is Irregular Vol. 1
~ Parenting Teenage Werewolves
The Meter is Irregular Vol. 2
~ Unleashing Teenage Werewolves
The Meter is Irregular Vol. 3
~ Inner Life of Turtles
The Meter is Irregular Vol. 4 *~ Colorfast*
The Meter is Irregular Vol. 5 *~ Colorfast: Part 2*